Made in the USA
Monee, IL
29 March 2023

30798370R00070